THE
GREAT AMERICAN
PEANUT BUTTER BOOK

★★★★★★★★★★★★★★★★★★★★★★★★★★★★

D1502025

THE
GREAT AMERICAN
PEANUT BUTTER BOOK

★★★★★★★★★★★★★★★★★★★★★★★★★★★★

*A Book of Recipes, Facts,
Figures, and Fun*

LARRY AND HONEY
ZISMAN

St. Martin's Press ★ New York

THE GREAT AMERICAN PEANUT BUTTER BOOK.
Copyright © 1985 by Honey and Larry Zisman. All rights reserved. Printed in the
United States of America. No part of this book may be used or reproduced in any
manner whatsoever without written permission except in the case of brief quotations
embodied in critical articles or reviews. For information, address St. Martin's Press,
175 Fifth Avenue, New York, N.Y. 10010.

Design by Laura Hough

Library of Congress Cataloging in Publication Data

Zisman, Larry.
    The great American peanut butter book.

    1. Cookery (Peanut butter)   I. Zisman, Honey.
II. Title.
TX814.5.P38Z57   1985   641.6′56596   85–1779
ISBN 0–312–34481–3 (pbk.)

First Edition

10 9 8 7 6 5 4 3 2 1

for JORDANA and CRAIG
who never met a jar of peanut butter
they didn't like

CONTENTS

★★★★★★★★★★★★★★★★★★★★★★★★★

INTRODUCTION

★★★★★★★★★★★★★★★★★★★★★★★★★

We like peanut butter and we like it a lot.

How much do we like it?

Would you believe that in the United States we eat close to 700 million pounds of peanut butter each year?

How much, you ask, is 700 million pounds?

Well, for starters, that's more than the weight of seven ocean liners the size of the *Titanic*.

Or, picture, if you can:

A tower of 18-ounce jars of peanut butter standing nearly 52,000 miles high, more than one fifth of the distance from the earth to the moon

Those same jars of peanut butter standing side by side, forming a low wall stretching 32,000 miles, almost one and one third times around the world at the equator

A football field covered with peanut butter to a height of 225 feet

But, seriously, how much peanut butter is 700 million pounds?
Enough to make 10 billion peanut butter and jelly sandwiches with two tablespoons of peanut butter in each sandwich.

And, that, fellow peanut butter lovers, is a lot of peanut butter.

A peanut sat on the railroad track,
His heart was all a flutter,
Along came a train, the 5:15,
Toot, toot, peanut butter.

PRIVATE-LABEL PEANUT BUTTER—IT'S EASY TO MAKE YOUR OWN

★★★★★★★★★★★★★★★★★★★★★★★★★★★★★

It's easy, fast, and a lot of fun to make your own peanut butter at home. All you need is a regular kitchen blender.

Put 2 cups of peanuts—either fresh out of the shell or dry roasted from the jar—in a blender and add 1 or 2 tablespoons peanut oil. Run the blender at its highest speed until the peanuts have become peanut butter. Stop the blender two or three times and scrape down the sides to make sure that all the peanuts get blended into peanut butter.

If you want, you can add to the blender a little salt and a little sugar to suit your taste. And if you prefer chunky rather than smooth, just stir some coarsely chopped pieces of peanuts into your peanut butter after you have taken it out of the blender.

Regular peanut butter can be stored either in the refrigerator or on a shelf at room temperature. Keeping it in the refrigerator will make it last a few months longer (if it does not get eaten first), but the peanut butter will be harder to spread if you do not take it out half an hour or so before eating it.

If it gets very hot and humid where you live, it is better to keep old-fashioned or natural peanut butter in the refrigerator. Oil separation in this type of peanut butter can be prevented by storing the jar upside down.

RIGHT OUT OF THE JAR—HOW TO ENJOY PEANUT BUTTER WITHOUT ANY WORK

★★★★★★★★★★★★★★★★★★★★★★★★★★★★★★

A spoonful of peanut butter right out of the jar is a delicious and nutritious treat, and it is comforting to know that there are many, many other ways to enjoy peanut butter with very little work and not just spreading it on a slice of bread.

For quick and easy enjoyment of peanut butter, have it:

- stirred into a dish of chocolate pudding
- daubed on popcorn
- spread on carrots and celery sticks
- on top of hot apple pie
- scooped up with pretzels
- blended into a banana daiquiri
- as a topping for sweet potatoes
- spread on cinnamon toast
- stirred into coffee or hot chocolate
- mixed into yogurt
- dipped up with a breadstick
- along with chocolate chips
- on a corn muffin
- carefully spread on potato chips and corn chips
- scooped up with Chinese noodles
- spread on pork chops or baked ham
- covering a graham cracker

- mixed into baked beans
- on Melba toast
- spread on corn on the cob
- on a sourdough biscuit
- coating a granola bar
- as a dip for breaded onion rings
- along with a jelly doughnut
- added to a bowl of cereal
- daubed on orange slices
- on top of brownies
- combined with cottage cheese
- on a slice of banana bread
- as a dip for fried chicken
- mixed into applesauce
- coating a candy bar
- added to macaroni and cheese
- spread on Oreo cookies
- as a topping for waffles, pancakes, or French toast
- on a croissant
- spread on a piece of matzoh
- on top of baked potatoes or mashed potatoes
- along with layer cake
- mixed into macaroni salad or potato salad

- stirred into a bowl of ice cream
- spread on Fig Newtons
- daubed on a half of a broiled grapefruit
- mixed into chili
- spread on angel food cake
- stirred into hot cooked cereal
- as a topping for string beans
- dipped up with licorice sticks

It's nice to know that peanut butter is one of those rare foods that not only tastes good but also is good for you.

According to Consumer Reports magazine, which is usually restrained in its praise of the products it tests, peanut butter is a "convenient, nutritious, inexpensive food that appeals to many tastes."

Indeed, peanut butter is a very nutritious food. Two tablespoons of peanut butter—the amount used for a regular-sized sandwich—gives the following percentages of a seven- to ten-year-old's recommended daily allowances for vitamins and minerals:

Vitamin B_6	10%	Niacin	35%
Iron	10%	Phosphorous	20%
Magnesium	25%	Protein	30%
Zinc	10%		

Comparing peanut butter to other lunchtime servings, peanut butter has:

- more protein than chicken salad, egg salad, boiled ham, or bologna
- more niacin than cottage cheese, hamburger, milk, or eggs
- more iron than cottage cheese
- more thiamine than cottage cheese or tuna
- more phosphorus than milk or eggs
- more magnesium than tuna
- more Vitamin D than hamburger
- as much fiber as a slice of whole-wheat bread

In addition, for people on restricted diets, peanut butter has no cholesterol and very little salt.

PB&J AND MUCH, MUCH MORE—GREAT SANDWICH IDEAS

★★★★★★★★★★★★★★★★★★★★★★★★★★★★

In addition to the all-time favorite sandwich of peanut butter and jelly, there are many other kinds of peanut butter sandwiches.

Whether you use white bread, toast, rye bread with seeds, raisin bread, pita bread, a bialy, Italian bread, black bread, whole-wheat bread, a hot dog roll, Indian chapati bread, pumpernickel bread, an English muffin, a hamburger roll, Swedish limpa bread, a bagel, rye bread without seeds, challah bread, or French bread, make yourself a sandwich with peanut butter and:

- cream cheese
- hard boiled egg and pimiento
- apple slices
- tuna
- chopped prunes
- bologna and sweet relish
- a hamburger
- sliced bananas
- alfalfa sprouts and sunflower seeds
- Canadian bacon
- cranberry sauce
- roasted chestnuts
- cucumber and watercress
- molasses
- bacon
- deviled ham
- flaked coconut and sesame seeds
- minute steak
- grilled cheese
- chopped cherries and pecans
- ham and cheese
- sloppy joe ingredients
- zucchini and bean sprouts
- salami and onion
- breaded veal cutlet and parsley

- marshmallow creme
- tofu
- sausage
- chopped liver and radishes
- honey and walnuts
- raisins and grated carrot
- chicken
- liverwurst
- mushrooms and caviar
- avocado
- lettuce, tomato, and mayonnaise
- a hot dog
- olives
- dates
- breaded fish fillet

The U.S. Food and Drug Administration has very specific regulations concerning what is peanut butter and what is not. Any product labeled "peanut butter" must have at least 90 percent peanuts and may contain only the following additives: salt, sugar, sucrose, dextrose, or hydrogenated fat or oil as an emulsifier to prevent the peanut oil from separating and rising to the top and to ensure its spreading easily without tearing your bread.

No artificial flavorings, artificial sweeteners, chemical preservatives, colorings, or animal fats are allowed.

Any peanut spread that does not conform to these standards must be labeled "imitation peanut butter."

"VIPB"—VERY IMPORTANT PEANUT BUTTER RECIPES

★★★★★★★★★★★★★★★★★★★★★★★★★★★★

JIMMY CARTER'S PEANUT BUTTER PIE

★★★★★★★★★★★★★★★★★★★★★★★★★★★★

(SPECIAL THANKS TO PRESIDENT JIMMY CARTER)

1 package (8 ounces) cream cheese
1 cup of 4x sugar
¼ cup crunchy peanut butter
½ cup milk
¼ cup of peanuts (halves)
1 container (9 ounces) Cool Whip

Whip cream cheese until soft and fluffy, beat in peanut butter and sugar, slowly add milk, fold in Cool Whip. Put into graham cracker pie crusts, sprinkle tops with peanuts, then freeze.

Makes 2 pies

According to many surveys, peanut butter and jelly is the most popular kind of sandwich in the United States.

ANNETTE FUNICELLO'S PEANUT BUTTER COOKIES

★★★★★★★★★★★★★★★★★★★★★★★★★★

(SPECIAL THANKS TO ANNETTE FUNICELLO AND SKIPPY PEANUT BUTTER)

2 cups unsifted flour

1 cup sugar

1/2 teaspoon baking soda

1/4 teaspoon salt

1/2 cup corn oil margarine, softened

1/2 cup Skippy creamy or super chunk
peanut butter

2 eggs

1 tablespoon water

1 teaspoon vanilla

In small bowl stir together flour, sugar, baking soda, and salt. In large bowl with mixer at low speed beat together margarine, peanut butter, eggs, water, and vanilla just until blended. Add flour mixture; beat until blended. Increase speed to medium; beat 2 minutes. Drop by rounded tablespoonfuls 3 inches apart onto ungreased cookie sheets. Flatten slightly with floured bottom of glass. Bake in 375° F oven 10 to 12 minutes or until lightly browned. Cool on wire rack. Store in tightly covered container.

Makes about 3 dozen

PEANUT BUTTER CHOCOLATE CHIP COOKIES

Stir 1 package (6 ounces) semisweet chocolate pieces into batter.

PEANUT BUTTER OAT COOKIES

Decrease flour to 1 cup. Add 1 cup quick oats.

Kentucky artist C. G. Morehead painted a rural scene using oil pigments mixed in a base of peanut butter. The painting was autographed by President Jimmy Carter—no stranger to peanuts himself—and sold for $10,500, which was donated to a program to help handicapped children.

SESAME FRUIT AND NUT SQUARES

★★★★★★★★★★★★★★★★★★★★★★★★★★★

(SPECIAL THANKS TO SKIPPY PEANUT BUTTER)

3/4 cup unsifted flour
1/2 teaspoon baking soda
1/4 teaspoon baking powder
Dash salt
1/4 cup corn oil margarine
1/4 cup Skippy creamy or super chunk
   peanut butter
1/2 cup (packed) brown sugar
1 egg
1/2 cup chopped dried mixed fruit or raisins
1/4 cup sesame seeds

Grease 8 × 8 × 2-inch baking pan. In small bowl stir together flour, baking soda, baking powder, and salt. In large bowl with mixer at medium speed beat together margarine, peanut butter, sugar, and egg until smooth. With wooden spoon, stir in flour mixture, fruit, and sesame seeds. Spread in prepared pan. Bake in 350° F oven 15 to 18 minutes, or until cake tester inserted in center comes out clean. (Entire surface will be lightly browned.)

Makes 16 (2-inch) squares

PETER PAN'S POPCORN CAKE

★★★★★★★★★★★★★★★★★★★★★★★★★★

(SPECIAL THANKS TO PETER PAN PEANUT BUTTER)

> 3/4 cup Peter Pan peanut butter, creamy or
>   crunchy
> 5 cups miniature marshmallows
> 1/2 cup butter or margarine
> 5 quarts popped popcorn
> 1 pound plain chocolate candies, gum drops,
>   or mixture of chocolate chips and peanut
>   butter chips
> 1 cup salted peanuts

Combine peanut butter, marshmallows, and butter in 2-quart saucepan. Cook over low heat until melted, stirring constantly. Combine popcorn, plain chocolate candies, and peanuts in large mixing bowl. Pour marshmallow mixture over popcorn and mix well. Press firmly into well-buttered 10-inch tube pan, or spread in greased 9 × 13-inch pan. Chill until firm. Slice with bread knife.

PEANUT BUTTER DATE COOKIES

★★★★★★★★★★★★★★★★★★★★★★★★★★★

(SPECIAL THANKS TO SUPERMAN PEANUT BUTTER)

4 cups sifted all-purpose flour
1 teaspoon baking powder
1/4 teaspoon baking soda
1 teaspoon salt
1/2 teaspoon ground cinnamon
1/4 teaspoon ground nutmeg
1 cup Superman Crunchy Peanut Butter
1 cup butter or margarine
1 cup (packed) brown sugar
2/3 cup granulated sugar
2 eggs
1 cup chopped dates

Sift together flour, baking powder, soda, salt, and spices. Cream peanut butter and butter. Gradually stir in sugars and beat until light and fluffy. Beat in eggs, one at a time; then mix in flour mixture. Stir in dates. Shape into 4 8-inch rolls. Wrap with waxed paper or plastic wrap. Chill thoroughly. Cut into thin slices, place on ungreased baking sheet, and bake at 400° F for 5 to 8 minutes.

Makes 7 dozen

Note: Unbaked dough may be stored in refrigerator for several weeks.

Political commentator, analyst, pundit, author, columnist, and television show host William F. Buckley, Jr., is a true peanut butter enthusiast. When he first got married he told his wife that he expected peanut butter for breakfast every day, and once, when he listed his life values, peanut butter was ranked fifth, after God, family, country, and J. S. Bach but ahead of Yale and good English prose. And in one of his columns Mr. Buckley wrote the following couplet:

> *I know that I shall never see*
> *A poem as lovely as Skippy's*
> *peanut butter*

NUTTY STREUSEL-FILLED CAKE

★★★★★★★★★★★★★★★★★★★★★★★★★★★★

(COURTESY OF THE PROCTER & GAMBLE COMPANY)

1 package golden pound cake mix
1/3 cup all-purpose flour
1/3 cup sugar
1/2 cup Jif Crunchy Peanut Butter
Peanut Butter Glaze

Preheat oven to 325° F. Prepare cake mix according to package directions. Turn half the batter into a greased and floured 8½-inch fluted tube pan. Combine flour and sugar. Cut in Jif until mixture resembles coarse crumbs. Sprinkle over batter in pan; top with remaining batter. Bake in 325° F oven for 50 to 55 minutes. Cool in pan 10 minutes. Remove from pan; cool on wire rack. Drizzle with Peanut Butter Glaze. Garnish with strawberries, if desired.

PEANUT BUTTER GLAZE

In mixing bowl, combine 1 cup sifted powdered sugar, 2 tablespoons milk, 1 tablespoon Jif Creamy Peanut Butter, and ½ teaspoon vanilla. Mix till smooth.

PEANUT BUTTER LOG

★★★★★★★★★★★★★★★★★★★★★★★★

(SPECIAL THANKS TO DEAF SMITH OLD FASHIONED PEANUT BUTTER)

1 cup peanut butter
1 cup raw honey
1 1/2–2 cups non-instant non-fat dry milk
1 teaspoon pure vanilla
Dash of salt (optional)

Mix all ingredients; knead until thoroughly blended; form a log and roll in chopped nuts or wheat germ; slice to serve. Store in refrigerator. Freezes well for serving later.

Note: Instant non-fat dry milk will not work.

24 slices

PEANUT BUTTER AND POTATO CHIP COOKIES

★★★★★★★★★★★★★★★★★★★★★★★★★★★★

(SPECIAL THANKS TO LAURA SCUDDER'S PEANUT BUTTER)

> 2 cups brown sugar
> 1/2 cup shortening
> 2 eggs
> 1 3/4 cups flour
> 1 teaspoon baking soda
> 3/4 cup Laura Scudder's Peanut Butter
> 1 teaspoon vanilla
> 1 cup (2 ounces) Laura Scudders Potato
>   Chips (crushed)
> 1 cup (2 1/2 ounces) Laura Scudder's diced
>   walnuts
> Optional: 1 package (11 1/2 ounces)
>   chocolate drops

1. Cream sugar, shortening, and eggs.
2. Add peanut butter.
3. Add flour, soda, and vanilla. Mix well. (Dough will be somewhat stiff.)

4. Blend in potato chips and walnuts. Add chocolate drops if desired.
5. Drop by heaping teaspoonfuls onto ungreased cookie sheet.
6. Bake at 350° F for 10 to 12 minutes.
7. Remove from cookie sheet and allow to cool on rack before storing.

Makes approximately 4 dozen

When peanut butter was in short supply because of the 1980 summer drought that reduced the peanut crop, many families stocked up on peanut butter because they feared that there would be none available in the stores. Jake Bender, the manager of Randalls Foods supermarket in Dubuque, Iowa, told Newsweek magazine, "I'll bet there are houses in this town with fifty jars of peanut butter stored away."

FROZEN YOGURT SQUARES
★★★★★★★★★★★★★★★★★★★★★★★★★★★★★
(SPECIAL THANKS TO ADAMS OLD FASHIONED PEANUT BUTTER)

1 1/2 cups graham cracker crumbs
3 tablespoons sugar
1/3 cup butter or margarine, melted
4 cartons (8 ounces each) plain yogurt
1/3 cup honey
1 teaspoon grated orange rind
1 cup Adams Old Fashioned Peanut Butter

Combine . . . . . crumbs and sugar in bowl.

Add . . . . butter. Stir with fork until well blended.

Reserve. . . . . . 1/4 cup crumbs for topping. Press remaining crumbs into 9-inch square pan.

Combine . . . . . yogurt, honey, and orange rind in bowl. Mix well.

Swirl. . . . . peanut butter into yogurt mixture with rubber scraper.

Pour . . . . yogurt mixture over crumbs in pan. Sprinkle with reserved crumbs.

Cover . . . . with foil and freeze overnight. Let stand about 30 minutes before cutting and serving.

Makes 12 servings

28

FROSTED PEANUT BUTTER BARS

★★★★★★★★★★★★★★★★★★★★★★★★★★★

(SPECIAL THANKS TO THE PEANUT ADVISORY BOARD)

Creamy peanut butter—1 cup
Butter or margarine—²/3 cup
Granulated sugar—1¹/2 cups
Light brown sugar—1¹/2 cups

1. In mixer bowl, blend peanut butter and butter until creamy. Gradually beat in sugars.

Eggs, beaten—6
Vanilla—2 teaspoons

2. Add eggs gradually; beat well after each addition. Beat in vanilla.

All-purpose flour—1 pound
Baking powder—4 teaspoons
Salt—¹/2 teaspoon
Peanut granules—1 cup

3. Combine flour, baking powder, and salt. Stir in peanut butter mixture and granules.
4. Spread into greased 12 × 20 × 2-inch pan. Bake in 350° F oven for 30 minutes. Cool in pan.

FROSTING

Creamy peanut butter—$^2/_3$ cup
Vanilla—2 teaspoons
Milk—$^2/_3$ cup
Confectioners sugar—5 cups

1. Beat together peanut butter and vanilla.
2. Gradually add milk and sugar; beat after each addition.
3. Beat until spreading consistency. Frost cooled bars; cut into 24 pieces.

Serving: 1 piece about $1^1/_2 \times 3$ inches

Senator Barry Goldwater of Arizona once ran out of shaving cream while on a camping trip, so he used peanut butter as a substitute. "It's a darn good lotion," he said, "if you don't mind smelling like a peanut."

PEANUT BUTTER COOKIES—YOU CAN'T STOP AFTER EATING JUST ONE

★★★★★★★★★★★★★★★★★★★★★★★★★★★★★

PEANUT BUTTER CRISSCROSS COOKIES

★★★★★★★★★★★★★★★★★★★★★★★★★★

1 cup shortening
1 cup peanut butter
1 cup granulated sugar
1 cup (packed) brown sugar
2 eggs
1 teaspoon vanilla
2¹/₂ cups all-purpose flour
1 teaspoon baking soda
Dash salt

Preheat oven to 400° F.

Cream together shortening and peanut butter. Gradually add sugars, blending well. Add eggs, one at a time, beating until smooth. Add vanilla. Set aside.

Combine flour, baking soda, and salt. Stir into peanut butter mixture.

Using dampened hands, shape batter into 1-inch balls and place 2 inches apart on a greased cookie sheet. Flatten with a fork in a crosscross pattern, then bake for about 8 minutes.

Yield: Approximately 6 dozen cookies

FUDGIE SQUARES

★★★★★★★★★★★★★★★★★★★★★★★★★★★

1 cup plus 2 tablespoons softened butter or
*   margarine*
2 cups brown sugar
2 eggs
2/3 cup peanut butter
1 tablespoon vanilla
1 1/2 cups all-purpose flour
1 teaspoon baking soda
Dash salt
3 cups quick oat cereal
2 cups semisweet chocolate chips
1 can (14 ounces) sweetened condensed
*   milk*
1 cup chopped nuts

Preheat oven to 350° F.

Mix together the 1 cup butter and the sugar. Beat in eggs, peanut butter, and vanilla. Set aside.

Combine flour, baking soda, and salt. Add quick oat cereal. Stir into peanut butter mixture. Set aside.

Combine chocolate chips, milk, and the 2 tablespoons butter and melt over hot water, stirring until smooth and well blended. Stir in chopped nuts. Set aside.

Spread peanut butter mixture evenly in a greased 9 × 13-inch pan. Spoon chocolate mixture over top. Bake for 25 to 30 minutes.

Let cool completely and cut into 2-inch squares.

Yield: Approximately 2 dozen squares

Peanut butter sticks to the roof of your mouth because of a process called "hydration of the peanut protein." In plain words, the high level of protein in peanut butter draws the moisture away from your mouth as you eat it just like a sponge soaks up water.

CRUNCH AND RAISIN COOKIES

★★★★★★★★★★★★★★★★★★★★★★★★★

1 3/4 cups all-purpose flour
1 teaspoon baking soda
1/4 teaspoon salt
1/2 cup softened butter or margarine
1/2 cup peanut butter
1 cup granulated sugar
1 cup (packed) light brown sugar
2 eggs
1/4 cup milk
1 teaspoon vanilla
2 1/2 cups granola
1 cup raisins

Preheat oven to 350° F.

Combine flour, baking soda, and salt. Set aside.

Cream together butter, peanut butter, and sugars. Beat in eggs, milk, and vanilla. Stir in flour mixture, granola, and raisins.

Drop by teaspoonfuls about 3 inches apart on a greased cookie sheet. Bake for about 15 minutes, until lightly browned.

Yield: Approximately 4 dozen cookies

PECAN MERINGUE DROPS

★★★★★★★★★★★★★★★★★★★★★★★★★

2 egg whites
1/8 teaspoon cream of tartar
2/3 cup granulated sugar
1 teaspoon vanilla
Dash salt
1/2 cup chopped pecans
1/2 cup creamy peanut butter

Preheat oven to 300° F.

Beat together egg whites and cream of tartar until stiff peaks form. Gradually beat in sugar and continue beating until very stiff peaks form. Gently mix in vanilla, salt, pecans, and peanut butter.

Drop by teaspoonfuls onto a greased cookie sheet. Bake for 25 minutes, until lightly browned.

Remove immediately from cookie sheet.

Yield: Approximately 3 dozen cookies

It takes about 720 peanuts to make 1 pound of peanut butter.

CHUNKY BROWNIES

★★★★★★★★★★★★★★★★★★★★★★★★★★★★

1/2 cup softened butter or margarine
1 cup granulated sugar
1 teaspoon vanilla
2 eggs
1 1/4 cups all-purpose flour
1/4 teaspoon baking soda
3/4 cup chocolate syrup
1/2 cup chunky peanut butter
Chunky Frosting (recipe follows)

Preheat oven to 350° F.

Cream together butter, sugar, and vanilla. Add eggs, beating well. Set aside.

Combine flour and baking soda. Add, alternately with chocolate syrup, to butter mixture. Stir in peanut butter.

Pour batter into a greased 9 × 13-inch pan. Bake for 30 to 35 minutes.

Let cool in pan and top with frosting. Cut into 2-inch squares.

Yield: Approximately 2 dozen squares

CHUNKY FROSTING

⅓ *cup granulated sugar*
¼ *cup evaporated milk*
2 *tablespoons butter or margarine*
½ *cup chunky peanut butter*
1 *teaspoon vanilla*

Combine sugar, milk, and butter in a saucepan and cook over medium heat, stirring constantly, until mixture boils.

Remove from heat and immediately stir in peanut butter and vanilla. Beat mixture until smooth.

The head of a private school for girls in South Africa banned peanut butter from the school campus because she believed that it sexually stimulated the students.

COFFEE SPARKLERS

★★★★★★★★★★★★★★★★★★★★★★★★★★

1 cup brown sugar
1/2 cup oil
1 egg
1 cup peanut butter
1 teaspoon very strong coffee
1 1/2 cups all-purpose flour
1/4 teaspoon salt
1/2 teaspoon baking soda

Preheat oven to 375° F.

Mix together brown sugar and oil. Beat in egg. Add peanut butter and coffee, mixing well. Set aside.

Combine flour, salt, and baking soda and add to peanut butter mixture, blending well.

Shape batter into 1-inch balls and place on a greased cookie sheet. Flatten with the bottom of a dampened glass that has been dipped in sugar. Bake for about 10 minutes, until golden brown.

Yield: Approximately 4 dozen cookies

PB & JAM COOKIES

★★★★★★★★★★★★★★★★★★★★★★★★★★

1/2 cup softened butter or margarine
1/2 cup granulated sugar
1/2 cup brown sugar
1 egg (2 eggs if peanut butter is very dry)
1 cup peanut butter
1/2 teaspoon salt
1/2 teaspoon baking soda
1 teaspoon vanilla
1 1/4 cups all-purpose flour
Jam

Preheat oven to 350° F.

Cream butter and sugars. Beat in egg(s), peanut butter, salt, and baking soda. Add vanilla. Gradually add flour and mix until well blended.

Using slightly greased hands, shape dough into 1-inch balls and place on a greased cookie sheet. Flatten with a fork.

Place a small amount of jam on top of each cookie and bake for 12 to 15 minutes.

Yield: Approximately 3 dozen cookies

CHOCOLATE BUTTERSCOTCH SQUARES

★★★★★★★★★★★★★★★★★★★★★★★★★

2 cups all-purpose flour
2 cups (packed) brown sugar
1 teaspoon baking powder
1/2 teaspoon baking soda
1 cup peanut butter
1/2 cup softened butter or margarine
1 cup milk
3 eggs
1 teaspoon vanilla
1 cup milk chocolate chips
1 cup butterscotch chips

Preheat oven to 350° F.

Mix together flour, sugar, baking powder, and baking soda. Add peanut butter and butter, blending until mixture becomes crumbly. Set aside 1 cup of mixture.

Add milk, eggs, and vanilla to remaining peanut butter mixture, blending well.

Pour batter into a 9 × 13-inch pan. Sprinkle chocolate chips and butterscotch chips over batter. Sprinkle remaining cup of peanut butter mixture over top. Bake for 40 to 45 minutes, until toothpick tests clean.

Let cool and cut into 2-inch squares.

Yield: Approximately 2 dozen squares

National Peanut Week was first observed in 1941. In 1974 it was expanded to become National Peanut Month, celebrated each year during March. As part of the festivities, the United States Senate restaurant adds peanut soup to its menu, and Baskin-Robbins serves peanut-butter-and-jelly-flavored ice cream.

The restaurants belonging to Chicago's Fine Dining Association mark the occasion by featuring specially created original recipes using peanut butter, including roast duck with peanut sauce at Arnie's, peanut soup at That Steak Joynt, and peanut salad dressing at Truffles.

POWDERED WALNUT BROWNIES

★★★★★★★★★★★★★★★★★★★★★★★★★★★★

1/2 cup all-purpose flour
Dash salt
1/2 cup peanut butter
1/4 cup softened butter or margarine
1 teaspoon vanilla
1 cup (packed) brown sugar
2 eggs
1 cup chopped walnuts
Confectioners sugar

Preheat oven to 350° F.

Combine flour and salt. Set aside.

Cream together peanut butter, butter, and vanilla. Gradually add brown sugar, blending well. Add eggs, one at a time, beating well. Mix in flour mixture and walnuts.

Spoon batter evenly into a greased 8-inch square pan. Bake for 30 to 45 minutes, until firm.

Let cool slightly and sprinkle confectioners sugar over top. Cut into 2-inch squares.

Yield: Approximately 16 squares

OAT AND BANANA GOODIES

★★★★★★★★★★★★★★★★★★★★★★★★★

1 1/2 cups all-purpose flour
1/2 teaspoon baking powder
1/2 teaspoon salt
1 teaspoon ground cinnamon
1/4 teaspoon ground nutmeg
1/2 cup softened butter or margarine
1/2 cup chunky peanut butter
1 cup granulated sugar
1 egg
1 banana, mashed
1 1/2 cups quick oat cereal

Preheat oven to 375° F.

Combine flour, baking powder, salt, cinnamon, and nutmeg. Set aside.

Cream together butter, peanut butter, and sugar until light and fluffy. Beat in egg and banana. Gently fold in flour mixture and quick oat cereal.

Drop by teaspoonfuls onto a greased cookie sheet. Bake for 8 to 10 minutes.

Yield: Approximately 4 1/2 dozen cookies

Some statistics about peanut butter:

- Seventy percent of all the peanut butter sold is smooth and the remaining 30 percent is chunky
- Children generally prefer smooth over chunky, while the reverse is true for adults
- People on the West Coast like chunky better than smooth, while on the East Coast smooth is more popular
- On a per capita basis, Midwesterners eat the most peanut butter, while Southwesterners eat the least
- One third of all American children eat peanut butter at least twice a week
- Ten percent of the peanut butter eaten in this country is enjoyed at breakfast

COCONUT STRIPS

★★★★★★★★★★★★★★★★★★★★★★★★★★★

1 cup all-purpose flour
1 teaspoon baking powder
Dash salt
1/4 cup shortening
1 cup chunky peanut butter
1 cup granulated sugar
2 eggs, beaten
1 cup flaked coconut
1 teaspoon vanilla
Confectioners sugar

Preheat oven to 350° F.

Combine flour, baking powder, and salt. Set aside.

Cream together shortening and peanut butter. Gradually beat in sugar, then eggs. Stir in flour mixture, coconut, and vanilla.

Spread batter evenly in a greased 9 × 13-inch pan. Bake about 25 minutes.

Cut into 2 × 1/2-inch strips and sprinkle with confectioners sugar.

Yield: Approximately 6 dozen cookies

According to comedian Bill Cosby, "Man cannot live by bread alone. He must have peanut butter."

Peanut butter is the twelfth most purchased food item at supermarkets in the United States, with total sales amounting to nearly $1 billion each year.

HAVE YOUR (PEANUT BUTTER) CAKE AND EAT IT, TOO

★★★★★★★★★★★★★★★★★★★★★★★★★★★★★★★

CREAMY VELVET CAKE

★★★★★★★★★★★★★★★★★★★★★★★★★★

1/3 cup peanut oil
1 1/2 cups granulated sugar
1/2 cup creamy peanut butter
2 eggs
2 teaspoons unsweetened cocoa powder
2 1/4 cups all-purpose flour
1/2 teaspoon salt
1 cup buttermilk or 1 cup milk combined
*   with 1 tablespoon vinegar*
1 teaspoon vanilla
1 teaspoon baking soda
1 tablespoon vinegar
Creamy Velvet Icing (recipe follows)

Preheat oven to 350° F.

Mix together peanut oil, sugar, and peanut butter. Beat in eggs, one at a time. Mix in cocoa powder. Set aside.

Combine flour and salt and add, alternately with buttermilk, to peanut butter mixture. Stir in vanilla. Sprinkle baking soda and then vinegar over top and stir until well blended.

Pour batter into 3 greased and floured 9-inch cake pans. Bake for 30 to 35 minutes.

Let cool and cover layers and sides with icing.

CREAMY VELVET ICING

1 cup creamy peanut butter
1/2 cup softened butter or margarine
4 cups confectioners sugar
4 tablespoons very strong coffee

Cream together peanut butter and butter. Add sugar and coffee and beat until smooth.

Robert Golumb, a student at the Maryland Art Institute in Baltimore, made a real-life 2,000-pound peanut butter sandwich sculpture that was about the size of a double bed. He described the motivation for his work of art: "When I was a kid, I always wanted a peanut butter sandwich big enough to jump into."

SWIRL CAKE

★★★★★★★★★★★★★★★★★★★★★★★★★★

2 cups all-purpose flour
3/4 teaspoon salt
1 tablespoon baking powder
1/2 cup softened butter or margarine
1 cup granulated sugar
1/2 teaspoon vanilla
2 eggs
3/4 cup milk
1/2 cup peanut butter
2/3 cup chocolate syrup
Chocolate Peanut Butter Frosting (recipe
    follows)

Preheat oven to 350° F.

Combine flour, salt, and baking powder. Set aside.

Beat together butter and sugar until light and fluffy. Blend in vanilla. Beat in eggs, one at a time. Alternately add flour mixture and milk, beginning and ending with flour mixture, stirring well after each addition.

Stir peanut butter until it becomes soft. Add half of cake batter, mixing well. Stir chocolate syrup into remaining half of batter.

Alternately place large spoonfuls of light batter and dark batter in a greased 9 × 13-inch pan. Cut through batter several times with a knife, creating a marbled effect. Bake for 30 to 40 minutes.

Let cool and top with frosting.

CHOCOLATE PEANUT BUTTER FROSTING

1 cup semisweet chocolate chips
2 tablespoons softened butter or margarine
1/2 cup creamy peanut butter
1 teaspoon vanilla
2 1/2 cups confectioners sugar
1/2 cup evaporated milk
2 tablespoons light corn syrup

Melt chocolate chips over hot water, stirring until smooth. Remove from heat and blend in butter, peanut butter, and vanilla. Alternately add sugar and evaporated milk, stirring well after each addition. Stir in corn syrup.

SOUR CREAM CAKE

★★★★★★★★★★★★★★★★★★★★★★★★★★★

2 cups all-purpose flour
1 1/2 teaspoons baking powder
1/2 cup creamy peanut butter
1/2 cup softened butter or margarine
2 eggs
1 teaspoon vanilla
1 1/4 cups granulated sugar
1 cup sour cream
1 teaspoon baking soda
1 teaspoon ground cinnamon
1/2 cup chopped peanuts

Preheat oven to 350° F.

Combine flour and baking powder. Set aside.

Cream together peanut butter, butter, eggs, and vanilla. Add 1 cup of the sugar, the sour cream, and baking soda, mixing well. Stir in flour mixture.

Pour batter into a greased 9-inch springform pan.

Combine remaining 1/4 cup sugar, cinnamon, and chopped peanuts. Sprinkle over batter and work in slightly with a knife. Bake for 60 minutes.

A BERRY NICE CAKE
★★★★★★★★★★★★★★★★★★★★★★★★★★

1/2 cup softened butter or margarine
1 1/3 cups granulated sugar
1/2 cup chunky peanut butter
2 eggs
1 teaspoon vanilla
2 cups all-purpose flour
1 tablespoon baking powder
Dash salt
1 cup milk
1 1/2 cups raspberry jam
Creamy Icing (recipe follows)

Preheat oven to 350° F.

Cream together butter and sugar until light and fluffy. Mix in peanut butter, eggs, and vanilla. Set aside.

Combine flour, baking powder, and salt and add, alternately with milk, to peanut butter mixture, mixing well after each addition.

Pour batter into 2 greased 9-inch cake pans. Bake for 35 to 40 minutes, until toothpick tests clean.

Let cool for 10 minutes.

Remove from pan and cover top of 1 layer with raspberry jam. Place other layer on top and frost cake with icing.

CREAMY ICING

3 tablespoons softened cream cheese
1 tablespoon light corn syrup
1 1/4 cups confectioners sugar
1 teaspoon vanilla

Combine cream cheese and corn syrup. Add in sugar, beating until smooth. Mix in vanilla.

When professional tasters in the peanut butter industry taste different samples of peanut butter, they rinse their palates three times with water at 100 degrees and wait exactly 30 seconds in between samples. When doing these taste tests, a special utensil is used to pull a 1-tablespoon-sized plug of peanut butter from the exact center of the jar, assuring that the sample will not be from the sides or too near the top or bottom of the jar.

PB&P COFFEE CAKE
★★★★★★★★★★★★★★★★★★★★★★★★★

1/2 cup plus 3 tablespoons softened butter or
    margarine
1 cup granulated sugar
3 eggs
2 cups all-purpose flour
1/2 teaspoon salt
2 teaspoons baking powder
1 teaspoon grated lemon peel
1/2 cup milk
4 tablespoons chunky peanut butter
1/3 cup brown sugar
1/2 cup strawberry preserves
1/4 cup finely chopped peanuts
1 teaspoon ground cinnamon

Preheat oven to 350° F.

Cream together the 1/2 cup butter and 3/4 cup of the granulated sugar, beating until light and fluffy. Beat in eggs. Set aside.

Combine 1 3/4 cups of the flour, the salt, and baking powder. Set aside.

Combine lemon peel and milk. Add, alternately with flour mixture, to butter mixture, stirring well.

Pour batter into a greased 9-inch cake pan. Set aside.

Cream together the 3 tablespoons butter, peanut butter, brown sugar, and remaining ¼ cup flour. Spread evenly over batter.

Spoon strawberry preserves evenly over top. Set aside.

Combine remaining ¼ cup granulated sugar, peanuts, and cinnamon. Sprinkle over strawberry preserves. Bake for 40 to 45 minutes.

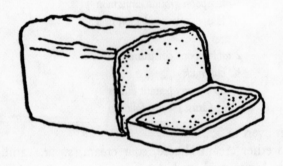

The scientific name for the fear of having peanut butter stick to the roof of your mouth is arachibutyrophobia.

PEANUT BUTTER CHEESECAKE

★★★★★★★★★★★★★★★★★★★★★★★★★

2 pounds softened cream cheese
1 cup sour cream
1 cup granulated sugar
2 teaspoons vanilla
1/4 teaspoon ground allspice
1/4 teaspoon ground cinnamon
1/4 teaspoon grated lemon peel
3 eggs
2 tablespoons cornstarch
1/2 cup milk
1 cup creamy peanut butter
Cake Crust (recipe follows)

Preheat oven to 350° F.

Mix together cream cheese, sour cream, sugar, vanilla, allspice, cinnamon, lemon peel, and eggs. Set aside.

Dissolve cornstarch in milk and add to cream cheese mixture. Blend in peanut butter.

Pour filling into crust. Bake for 60 to 65 minutes.

Let cool completely.

CAKE CRUST

3 cups all-purpose flour
1 cup softened butter or margarine
²/₃ cup granulated sugar
2 eggs

Combine flour, butter, sugar, and eggs, beating until smooth.
Press mixture onto bottom and sides of a 9-inch springform pan.

Olympic track athlete and setter of a world record for the indoor one-mile run, Dick Buerkle eats a great deal of peanut butter and says that it contributes to his performance as a runner.

PEANUT BUTTER SPICE CAKE

★★★★★★★★★★★★★★★★★★★★★★★★★★

2 1/4 cups all-purpose flour
1 1/4 cups granulated sugar
1 tablespoon baking powder
1/2 teaspoon salt
1 teaspoon ground cinnamon
1/4 teaspoon ground nutmeg
1/4 teaspoon ground cloves
2 eggs
1/3 cup shortening
1/2 cup chunky peanut butter
1 cup milk
*Coffee Peanut Butter Frosting (recipe
    follows)*

Preheat oven to 350° F.

Combine flour, sugar, baking powder, salt, cinnamon, nutmeg, and ground cloves, blending together well. Beat in eggs. Mix in shortening, peanut butter, and milk.

Pour batter into 2 greased and floured 9-inch cake pans. Bake for about 30 minutes, until toothpick tests clean.

Let cool and ice with frosting.

COFFEE PEANUT BUTTER FROSTING

1/2 cup peanut butter
1/4 cup very strong coffee
2 1/2 cups confectioners sugar
Dash salt
1 teaspoon vanilla
1/4 cup milk

Combine peanut butter, coffee, sugar, salt, vanilla, and milk, beating until smooth.

At the 1976 Democratic National Convention, where peanut farmer Jimmy Carter was nominated for President, the delegation from North Carolina displayed a sign that said "Peanut Butter is Love, Spread Some Around Today."

DIXIE DELIGHT

★★★★★★★★★★★★★★★★★★★★★★★★★★

1/2 cup softened butter or margarine
1/2 cup peanut oil
2 cups granulated sugar
5 egg yolks
2 cups all-purpose flour
1 teaspoon baking soda
1 cup buttermilk or 1 cup milk combined
  with 1 tablespoon vinegar
1 cup peanut butter
1 cup flaked coconut
5 egg whites, stiffly beaten
Dixie Delight Frosting (recipe follows)
1/2 cup chopped peanuts

Preheat oven to 350° F.

Combine butter, peanut oil, sugar, egg yolks, flour, baking soda, buttermilk, peanut butter, and coconut. Beat until well blended. Fold in egg whites.

Pour batter into 3 greased 9-inch cake pans. Bake for 25 minutes, until toothpick tests clean.

Let cool for 10 minutes, remove from pans, and let cool completely. Frost layers with frosting and sprinkle with chopped peanuts.

DIXIE DELIGHT FROSTING

8 ounces cream cheese
1/2 cup softened butter or margarine
4 cups confectioners sugar
1 teaspoon vanilla

Beat together cream cheese and butter until fluffy. Gradually add sugar and vanilla, mixing well.

Ellen E. Schaus and George M. Briggs, nutritionists at the University of California at Berkeley, evaluated forty commonly available foods to determine how good a consumer value they were on the basis of vitamins, minerals, and how much they cost. According to their study, the "best buy" foods include beef liver, wheat germ, eggs, carrots, and peanut butter.

APPLESAUCE 2-NUT SQUARES
★★★★★★★★★★★★★★★★★★★★★★★★★

1/2 cup chunky peanut butter
1 cup shortening
1 cup (packed) brown sugar
2 eggs
1/4 cup bran cereal
2/3 cup all-purpose flour
1/4 teaspoon salt
1 cup chopped walnuts
1/2 cup raisins
1 cup applesauce

Preheat oven to 350° F.

Cream together peanut butter, shortening, and sugar. Beat in eggs, one at a time. Set aside.

Combine bran cereal, flour, salt, chopped walnuts, and raisins. Mix into peanut butter mixture alternately with applesauce.

Pour batter into a greased 8-inch square pan. Bake for about 60 minutes.

Let cool slightly and cut into 2-inch squares.

Yield: Approximately 16 squares

PEANUT BUTTER PIES—AS AMERICAN AS THE APPLE KIND

★★★★★★★★★★★★★★★★★★★★★★★★★★★★★

PENNSYLVANIA DUTCH PB & MOLASSES PIE

★★★★★★★★★★★★★★★★★★★★★★★★★★

1 cup creamy peanut butter
1/2 cup all-purpose flour
1/2 cup (packed) brown sugar
2 tablespoons softened butter or margarine
1 teaspoon baking soda dissolved in 1 cup
    boiling water
2/3 cup light corn syrup
1/3 cup molasses
1 teaspoon vanilla
Graham Cracker Crust (recipe follows)

Preheat oven to 375° F.

Mix together peanut butter, flour, sugar, and butter. Set aside.

Mix together baking soda, corn syrup, molasses, and vanilla. Stir into peanut butter mixture.

Pour filling into graham cracker crust. Bake for 10 minutes. Reduce heat to 350° F and bake for 25 minutes longer, until filling is firm.

Let cool.

GRAHAM CRACKER CRUST

1 1/4 cups graham cracker crumbs
3 tablespoons granulated sugar
1/3 cup melted butter or margarine

Mix together graham cracker crumbs and sugar. Stir in butter. Press crust into a 9-inch pie pan.

CHOCOLATE MARSHMALLOW PIE

★★★★★★★★★★★★★★★★★★★★★★★★★★

5 cups marshmallows
1/2 cup milk
1 cup heavy cream, whipped, or frozen
   whipped topping, thawed
1/2 cup peanut butter
1 cup milk chocolate chips
Coconut Crust (recipe follows)

Combine marshmallows and milk and heat over hot water, stirring until mixture has melted and it is smooth and well blended.

Remove from heat and let cool. Add heavy cream, peanut butter, and chocolate chips, mixing well.

Spoon filling into crust.

COCONUT CRUST

2 tablespoons melted butter or margarine
2 cups flaked coconut

Preheat oven to 300° F.

Mix together butter and coconut and press into a 9-inch pie pan.
Bake for about 10 minutes, until golden brown.

One of America's great forgotten heroes is the unknown physician in
St. Louis in 1890 who, using his kitchen grinder, invented peanut
butter as a high protein, easily digestible food for his patients.

A short time after that, Dr. John Henry Kellogg, who later became
famous for his breakfast cereals, developed a peanut butter for his
patients at the Battle Creek Sanitarium, a health food retreat in
Michigan.

In 1903, Ambrose W. Straub of St. Louis received a patent for a
machine to make peanut butter. At the St. Louis World's Fair the
following year, with advertisements promoting the new health food rich
in protein, B vitamins, and minerals, the general public got its first
taste of peanut butter. It was an instant success with fairgoers, and
peanut butter quickly became a very popular food.

BANANA CREAM PIE

★★★★★★★★★★★★★★★★★★★★★★★★

2/3 cup granulated sugar
1/3 cup cornstarch
1/4 teaspoon salt
3 cups milk
4 egg yolks, lightly beaten
1/2 cup creamy peanut butter
2 bananas, sliced 1/4 inch thick
Meringue Crust (recipe follows)

Combine sugar, cornstarch, and salt in a saucepan. Gradually stir in milk and egg yolks.

Cook over medium heat, stirring constantly, until mixture thickens and comes to a boil. Boil for 1 minute.

Remove from heat and mix in peanut butter.

Cover surface of mixture with plastic wrap or wax paper to prevent skin from forming. Set aside to cool.

Arrange banana slices in meringue crust and spoon filling over top. Chill in the refrigerator until firm.

MERINGUE CRUST

3 egg whites, at room temperature
1½ cups granulated sugar
1½ teaspoons vanilla
1½ teaspoons vinegar
¼ cup boiling water

Preheat oven to 450° F.

Combine egg whites, sugar, vanilla, vinegar, and water. Beat about 10 to 12 minutes, scraping sides of bowl continuously, until stiff peaks form and mixture holds its shape.

Spoon crust into a 9-inch pie pan. Place crust in oven, turn off heat, and leave in oven for 4 to 5 hours without opening door.

The largest peanut butter manufacturing plant in the world is located in Dawson, Georgia, a small town of about 5,000 people in the southwestern part of the state, 150 miles due south of Atlanta. The factory, which is operated by Cargill, Inc., has the capacity to make 1 million pounds of peanut butter a week.

2-LAYER COCOA PIE

★★★★★★★★★★★★★★★★★★★★★★★★★

1 1/2 cups milk

2 1/2 teaspoons cornstarch

4 egg yolks

2/3 cup granulated sugar

1/4 ounce unflavored gelatin

1/2 cup creamy peanut butter

1 1/2 tablespoons unsweetened cocoa powder

4 egg whites, beaten to soft peaks

1 cup heavy cream, whipped, or frozen
    whipped topping, thawed

Chocolate–Graham Cracker Pie Crust
    (recipe follows)

1/2 cup chopped peanuts

Combine milk, cornstarch, egg yolks, and 1/3 cup of the sugar in a heavy saucepan. Sprinkle gelatin over top. Cook over low heat, stirring constantly, until mixture thickens and comes to a boil. Boil for 1 minute.

Remove from heat. Mix together 1 cup milk mixture and peanut butter. Chill in the refrigerator until firm.

Stir cocoa powder into remaining milk mixture. Chill in the refrigerator until firm.

Combine remaining $1/3$ cup sugar and egg whites, beating until stiff peaks form. Fold in half of the whipped cream and the peanut butter mixture. Set aside.

Spoon cocoa powder mixture evenly into pie crust. Spread peanut butter mixture over top. Chill in the refrigerator until firm.

Top with remaining whipped cream and peanuts to serve.

CHOCOLATE–GRAHAM CRACKER PIE CRUST

1 1/2 cups graham cracker crumbs
1/4 cup chocolate syrup
6 tablespoons chunky peanut butter

Preheat oven to 300° F.

Mix together graham cracker crumbs, chocolate syrup, and peanut butter.

Press crust into a 9-inch pie pan. Bake for 10 to 15 minutes, until crisp.

CHIFFON PIE

★★★★★★★★★★★★★★★★★★★★★★★★

2 egg yolks, beaten
3/4 cup granulated sugar
3/4 cup cold water
Dash salt
1/4 ounce unflavored gelatin, softened in 1/4
  cup water
1/2 cup creamy peanut butter
1 teaspoon vanilla
2 egg whites, beaten until foamy
Grape-Nuts Pie Crust (recipe follows)

Mix together egg yolks, 3/8 cup sugar, 1/4 cup of the cold water, and salt. Stir in softened gelatin.

Heat over boiling water, beating constantly, until mixture becomes thick and fluffy. Remove from heat and let cool.

Combine peanut butter and remaining 1/2 cup cold water, beating until well blended. Add egg yolk mixture and vanilla, mixing well. Chill in the refrigerator until slightly thickened.

Gradually add remaining 3/8 cup sugar to egg whites, beating until stiff peaks form. Fold into peanut butter mixture.

Spoon filling into pie crust. Chill in the refrigerator until firm.

GRAPE-NUTS PIE CRUST

1/2 cup crushed Grape-Nuts cereal
3 tablespoons maple syrup
6 tablespoons chunky peanut butter

Preheat oven to 300° F.

Mix together Grape-Nuts cereal, maple syrup, and peanut butter.
Press crust into a greased 9-inch pie pan.

Bake at 300° F for 10 to 15 minutes, until golden brown.

Prisoners in a jail in California went on strike because they wanted more peanut butter and jelly sandwiches. The strike ended after they received assurances that they would receive increased servings of their favorite sandwich.

HASTY PUDDINGS TO ENJOY SLOWLY

★★★★★★★★★★★★★★★★★★★★★★★★★★★★

TORTONI PUDDING

★★★★★★★★★★★★★★★★★★★★★★★★★★★

1/2 cup cookie crumbs
1/3 cup coarsely chopped peanuts
1/4 cup chocolate chips
3 3/4 ounces instant vanilla pudding mix
1 cup milk
1/4 cup plus 1 tablespoon granulated sugar
1 egg white, beaten foamy
1/3 cup creamy peanut butter
1 teaspoon instant coffee powder
1 teaspoon vanilla

Combine cookie crumbs, peanuts, and chocolate chips. Divide in half. Set aside.

Mix together vanilla pudding mix and milk. Set aside.

Gradually add 1 tablespoon sugar to egg white and beat until stiff peaks form. Stir in peanut butter, remaining 1/4 cup sugar, coffee powder, and vanilla. Mix in half of cookie crumb mixture.

Spoon into individual dessert dishes or wine glasses and sprinkle remaining cookie crumb mixture over top. Place in freezer until firm.

Yield: 6–8 servings

PEANUT BUTTER RICE PUDDING

★★★★★★★★★★★★★★★★★★★★★★★★★★★

3 eggs
³/₄ cup creamy peanut butter
¹/₂ cup granulated sugar
Dash salt
2 cups milk
2 cups cooked rice
¹/₂ cup chopped dates
Ground nutmeg

Preheat oven to 350° F.

Add eggs, one at a time, to peanut butter and mix well. Add sugar, salt, and milk, stirring until smooth. Stir in rice and dates.

Spoon pudding into a greased 1¹/₂ quart baking dish and sprinkle nutmeg over top. Place baking dish in a larger pan filled with 1 inch of water. Bake for about 1¹/₂ hours, until a knife placed midway between center and sides of baking dish tests clean.

Yield: 6–8 servings

FROZEN MOUSSE

★★★★★★★★★★★★★★★★★★★★★★★★★

½ cup creamy peanut butter
½ cup milk
Dash salt
¼ cup light corn syrup
¼ cup granulated sugar
1 egg white, beaten until foamy
1 cup heavy cream, whipped

Beat peanut butter and milk together until smooth. Add salt and corn syrup, blending well. Set aside.

Gradually add sugar to beaten egg white, beating constantly until mixture is smooth and shiny. Fold into whipped cream. Add peanut butter mixture, stirring well.

Pour into mold without stirring and freeze.

Remove from mold and let stand in the refrigerator for 1 hour before serving.

Yield: 6–8 servings

Peanut butter was included as a standard item in the snack pantry for the astronauts to eat on the Apollo moon flights.

Peanut butter devotees include gourmet cook Julia Child; actor Charlton Heston, who eats it by the plateful; author Dan Greenburg, who washes down his peanut butter sandwiches with champagne; and Ronald Davidson, the former executive chef at Sardi's restaurant in New York City, who would end each day with a glass of milk and a peanut butter and jelly sandwich.

I SCREAM, YOU SCREAM, WE ALL SCREAM FOR PEANUT BUTTER AND ICE CREAM

★★★★★★★★★★★★★★★★★★★★★★★★★★★★

CHOCOLATE OREO PEANUT BUTTER ICE CREAM

★★★★★★★★★★★★★★★★★★★★★★★★★★

1 can (14 ounces) sweetened condensed
  milk
2/3 cup chocolate syrup
1/2 cup peanut butter
1/2 cup chopped peanuts
1 cup crushed Oreo cookies
2 cups heavy cream, whipped

Combine milk, chocolate syrup, peanut butter, peanuts, and Oreo cookies, mixing together well. Gently stir in whipped cream.
Pour mixture into a 2-quart container and freeze overnight.

Yield: Approximately 1 1/2 quarts ice cream

About half of all the edible peanuts grown in the United States are made into peanut butter.

CRUNCHY PARFAIT

★★★★★★★★★★★★★★★★★★★★★★★★★★★★

³/₄ cup quick oat cereal
¹/₂ cup (packed) brown sugar
¹/₄ cup chopped peanuts
3 tablespoons melted butter or margarine
¹/₂ cup caramel topping
²/₃ cup creamy peanut butter
2 quarts softened strawberry ice cream or
*   ice milk*
Whipped cream (optional)

Preheat oven to 350° F.

Combine quick oat cereal, sugar, peanuts, and butter. Spread mixture in the bottom of a large baking pan. Bake for 10 to 15 minutes, stirring occasionally and watching closely to avoid burning.

Let cool completely and crumble. Set aside.

Mix together caramel topping, peanut butter, and ice cream. Freeze ice cream mixture until firm.

Spoon alternate layers of ice cream mixture and quick oat mixture into parfait glasses. Freeze until hard.

Serve with whipped cream, if desired.

Yield: 8–10 servings

PEANUT BUTTER PEACH ICE CREAM

★★★★★★★★★★★★★★★★★★★★★★★★★

2 egg yolks, beaten
2/3 cup granulated sugar
1 cup milk
1/2 cup creamy peanut butter
1/2 cup miniature marshmallows
1 cup mashed peaches
1 tablespoon apricot brandy
2 egg whites, stiffly beaten
1 cup heavy cream

Combine egg yolks, sugar, and milk in a saucepan and cook over medium heat, stirring constantly, until mixture thickens. Add peanut butter, mixing well. Add marshmallows and continue cooking, stirring constantly, until marshmallows have melted.

Remove from heat and stir in peaches and apricot brandy. Let cool for 15 minutes.

Fold in egg whites. Fold in heavy cream.

Pour mixture into a 5 × 9-inch loaf pan and cover with plastic wrap. Freeze until hard, stirring once every hour.

Yield: Approximately 1 quart ice cream

MOCHA PEANUT BUTTER MILK SHAKE

★★★★★★★★★★★★★★★★★★★★★★★★★★

4 tablespoons creamy peanut butter
2 cups milk
5 tablespoons chocolate syrup
3 scoops coffee ice cream or ice milk
1 tablespoon malted milk powder

Combine peanut butter, milk, chocolate syrup, ice cream, and malted milk powder in a blender and blend until thoroughly mixed.

Yield: 2 servings

Sam Bell, the long-time track coach at Indiana University, believes that peanut butter improves both the physical and the mental abilities of an athlete. The burst of energy provided by peanut butter makes an athlete, according to Coach Bell, "more positive and in higher spirits."

HONEY BANANA FROSTIE

★★★★★★★★★★★★★★★★★★★★★★★★★

1 banana
½ cup creamy peanut butter
2 cups milk
½ teaspoon ground cinnamon
2 tablespoons honey
3 scoops vanilla ice cream or ice milk

Combine banana, peanut butter, milk, cinnamon, honey, and ice cream in a blender and blend until thoroughly mixed.

Yield: 2 servings

The United States sells more peanut butter to Saudi Arabia than it sells to any other country in the world, and, in fact, Saudi Arabia buys twice as much as America's next best customer, Canada. Saudi Arabia now buys 150 times more peanut butter from this country than it bought ten years ago.

The Colorado Mine Company Restaurant in Denver, Colorado, offered a "Fool's Gold" sandwich: peanut butter, blueberry jam, and bacon on sourdough bread. The listed price was $18.95, more than the cost of the best steak in the house. However, the menu did note that the price of the sandwich was negotiable, with the waitress reportedly getting to keep for herself anything received over $5.00.

JUST DESSERTS—SAUCES THAT CAN'T BE TOPPED

★★★★★★★★★★★★★★★★★★★★★★★★★★★★★

PEANUT BUTTER HOT FUDGE SAUCE

★★★★★★★★★★★★★★★★★★★★★★★★★★★★

2½ ounces unsweetened chocolate
¾ cup milk
Dash salt
1 cup (packed) light brown sugar
1 teaspoon vanilla
4 tablespoons creamy peanut butter

Melt chocolate over hot water, stirring until smooth.

Combine chocolate, milk, salt, and sugar in a heavy saucepan. Cook over medium heat, stirring constantly, until sugar has dissolved.

Remove from heat. Add vanilla and peanut butter, mixing thoroughly.

Serve hot.

Yield: Approximately 1 cup of sauce

CHERRY APRICOT SAUCE

★★★★★★★★★★★★★★★★★★★★★★★★★★

1 cup apricot preserves
1/4 cup creamy peanut butter
1/2 cup chopped maraschino cherries

Combine apricot preserves, peanut butter, and maraschino cherries in a saucepan and cook over low heat, stirring constantly, until mixture is smooth and well blended.

Serve hot.

Yield: Approximately 1 1/2 cups of sauce

BEYOND REESE'S PEANUT BUTTER CUPS—MAKING YOUR OWN PEANUT BUTTER CANDY

★★★★★★★★★★★★★★★★★★★★★★★★★★★★★★★★

PEANUT BUTTER CHOCOLATE

★★★★★★★★★★★★★★★★★★★★★★★★★★★

2 cups semisweet chocolate chips
2 ounces unsweetened chocolate
1 cup chunky peanut butter
1/4 teaspoon salt
1 teaspoon vanilla

Melt chocolates over hot water, stirring until smooth. Remove from heat and mix in peanut butter, salt, and vanilla.

Spread mixture in a greased 8-inch square pan. Chill in the refrigerator until firm.

Cut into 1-inch squares.

Yield: Approximately 5 dozen squares

More peanut butter is eaten in the United States than all the jellies, jams, and preserves put together.

COCONUT BALLS

★★★★★★★★★★★★★★★★★★★★★★★★★

1 cup confectioners sugar
3/4 cup chunky peanut butter
1 egg, lightly beaten
1 cup flaked coconut
1/2 cup finely chopped peanuts
Dash salt
1 teaspoon vanilla

Mix together sugar and peanut butter. Beat in egg. Add coconut, peanuts, salt, and vanilla, mixing together well.

Using dampened hands, shape mixture into 1-inch balls.

Yield: Approximately 2 dozen candy balls

During the meat shortage in the United States during 1973 and 1974, consumers sought low-cost sources of protein, and the consumption of peanut butter went up by more than 15 percent.

CHOCOLATE-COATED CRUMBLES

★★★★★★★★★★★★★★★★★★★★★★★★★★★★

2 cups confectioners sugar
1 cup peanut butter
3/4 cup graham cracker crumbs
1/2 cup softened butter or margarine
1 cup semisweet chocolate chips
3 tablespoons shortening

Mix together sugar, peanut butter, graham cracker crumbs, and butter.

Using dampened hands, shape mixtures into 1-inch balls. Chill in the refrigerator until firm.

Combine chocolate chips and shortening and melt over hot water, stirring until mixture is smooth and well blended.

Dip candy balls into chocolate, coating completely. Place on a greased cookie sheet and chill in the refrigerator until coating is firm.

Yield: Approximately 3 dozen candy balls

CHEWIES

★★★★★★★★★★★★★★★★★★★★★★★★★★

1 cup dark corn syrup
1 cup granulated sugar
1 cup creamy peanut butter
1¼ cups peanuts
5 cups crisp rice cereal or any crispy cereal

Combine corn syrup and sugar in a large heavy saucepan and heat to boiling, stirring constantly.

Remove from heat and immediately stir in peanut butter. Add peanuts and cereal, mixing until well coated.

Press mixture into a greased 9 × 13-inch pan. Let cool and cut into 1-inch squares.

Yield: Approximately 8 dozen squares

WAFER CRUNCHIES

★★★★★★★★★★★★★★★★★★★★★★★★★★★★

2 cups granulated sugar
²/₃ cup milk
³/₄ cup vanilla wafer crumbs
¹/₂ cup finely chopped peanuts
1 teaspoon vanilla
¹/₂ cup peanut butter

Combine sugar and milk in a heavy saucepan and heat to boiling, stirring constantly. After sugar dissolves, continue to boil for 3 more minutes, still stirring.

Remove from heat and add vanilla wafer crumbs, peanuts, vanilla, and peanut butter. Stir until mixture thickens.

Drop by teaspoonfuls onto a greased cookie sheet. Chill in the refrigerator.

Yield: Approximately 2¹/₂ dozen candies

Champion golfer Al Geiberger was nicknamed the "Peanut Butter Kid" because he would always eat peanut butter and jelly sandwiches while playing in a tournament. He would keep a thick peanut butter and jelly sandwich in his golf bag and save it for when he needed extra energy on the later holes of a round or just before a crucial putt. Those sandwiches, Geiberger said, were his secret weapon.

CASTING PEANUT BUTTER IN A STARRING ROLL . . . AND IN BREADS, MUFFINS, AND BUNS

★★★★★★★★★★★★★★★★★★★★★★★★★★★★★★★

BANANA PEANUT BUTTER BREAD

★★★★★★★★★★★★★★★★★★★★★★★★★★

1/2 cup softened butter or margarine
1/2 cup granulated sugar
1/2 cup brown sugar
2 eggs
2 cups all-purpose flour
1/2 teaspoon salt
1/2 teaspoon baking soda
2 bananas, mashed
3/4 cup chunky peanut butter
1/2 cup chopped walnuts or pecans

Cream together butter and sugars. Add eggs, beating well. Set aside.

Combine flour, salt, and baking soda and stir, alternately with the mashed bananas, into the sugar mixture. Add peanut butter and chopped nuts, mixing well.

Pour batter into a greased 5 × 9-inch loaf pan and let stand at room temperature for 20 minutes.

Meanwhile, preheat oven to 325° F.

Bake for about 1 hour, until toothpick tests clean.

JAM SURPRISE MUFFINS

★★★★★★★★★★★★★★★★★★★★★★★★★★

1 3/4 cups all-purpose flour
2 1/2 teaspoons baking powder
2 1/2 tablespoons granulated sugar
1/4 teaspoon salt
1/4 cup softened butter or margarine
1/2 cup peanut butter
1 egg, beaten
3/4 cup milk
Jam

Preheat oven to 350° F.

Combine flour, baking powder, sugar, and salt. Mix in butter and peanut butter. Set aside.

Mix together egg and milk and stir into peanut butter mixture.

Spoon dough into muffin tins to fill three-fourths full. Put about 1/2 teaspoon of jam in center of each muffin, then bake for about 25 minutes, until golden brown.

Yield: Approximately 1 dozen muffins

SWEET ROLLS

★★★★★★★★★★★★★★★★★★★★★★★★★★★

1 cup boiling water
1 cup softened butter or margarine
1¼ cups granulated sugar
1 teaspoon salt
2 eggs
½ ounce active dry yeast dissolved in 1 cup
   warm water
6½ cups all-purpose flour
½ cup creamy peanut butter

Pour boiling water over butter, sugar, and salt in a bowl. Blend together well. Let cool slightly.

Add eggs, beating well. Mix in dissolved yeast and 3¼ cups flour, beating well. Stir in remaining 3¼ cups flour and peanut butter.

Chill in the refrigerator overnight.

Fill greased muffin tins three-fourths full with dough and let stand about 2 hours to let rise.

Preheat oven to 350° F.

Bake rolls for about 20 minutes, until golden brown.

Yield: Approximately 3 dozen rolls

HONEY DATE NUT BREAD

★★★★★★★★★★★★★★★★★★★★★★★★★

1/2 cup creamy peanut butter

2 tablespoons softened butter or margarine

3/4 cup honey

1 egg, beaten

1 teaspoon lemon juice

1/2 cup milk

1 1/2 cups all-purpose flour

1/4 teaspoon baking soda

Dash salt

1 teaspoon baking powder

2/3 cup chopped dates

2/3 cup chopped nuts

Preheat oven to 350° F.

Cream together peanut butter and butter. Mix in honey and egg. Set aside.

Add lemon juice to milk. Set aside.

Combine flour, baking soda, salt, and baking powder. Add, alternately with milk, to peanut butter mixture, beginning and ending with flour mixture. Stir in dates and nuts.

Pour dough into a greased 5 × 9-inch loaf pan. Bake for 50 to 60 minutes until toothpick tests clean.

One ounce of peanut butter provides enough energy for 20 minutes of swimming or 45 minutes of walking.

Basic Commodities Inc., a company in Clover, Wisconsin, that prepares lunches for school cafeterias, developed a machine that can make 100 peanut butter and jelly sandwiches a minute—or 6,000 an hour.

OATMEAL BREAD

★★★★★★★★★★★★★★★★★★★★★★★★★★

1 1/2 cups all-purpose flour
1 tablespoon baking powder
1/4 cup pecan meal or crushed Grape-Nuts
    cereal
1 cup granulated sugar
Dash salt
1/2 cup chunky peanut butter
1 cup quick oat cereal
1 egg, beaten
1 cup milk

Preheat oven to 350° F.

Combine flour, baking powder, pecan meal, sugar, and salt. Add peanut butter, mixing until crumbly. Stir in quick oat cereal, egg, and milk.

Spoon dough into a greased 5 × 9-inch loaf pan. Bake for about 50 minutes, until toothpick tests clean.

The most popular size jar of peanut butter sold is the 18-ounce jar.

PEANUT BUTTER ETCETERA—THE BEST OF THE REST

★★★★★★★★★★★★★★★★★★★★★★★★★★★★

PARTY MULTIMIX

★★★★★★★★★★★★★★★★★★★★★★★★★★

1 cup broken thin pretzel sticks
1 cup mixed nuts
1 cup broken corn chips
1/2 cup sunflower seeds
1/4 cup butter or margarine
1/2 cup creamy peanut butter
1/2 teaspoon ground cinnamon

Preheat oven to 350° F.

Combine pretzel sticks, nuts, corn chips, and sunflower seeds. Set aside.

Combine butter, peanut butter, and cinnamon in a saucepan and cook over low heat until mixture has melted and is smooth and well blended. Gradually pour over pretzel mix, stirring to coat evenly.

Put mixture into a 9 × 13-inch pan. Bake, stirring occasionally, for 10 to 12 minutes.

Let cool.

Yield: Approximately 4 cups of mix

SHERRY CHEESE BALLS

★★★★★★★★★★★★★★★★★★★★★★★★★★★

1 pound sharp cheddar, at room
   temperature, grated
3 ounces softened cream cheese
1/2 cup peanut butter
1/4 cup sherry
2 tablespoons mayonnaise
1/2 teaspoon garlic powder
1/4 teaspoon ground red pepper
1/2 cup chopped peanuts

Blend cheeses together. Mix in peanut butter, sherry, mayonnaise, garlic powder, and red pepper. Chill in refrigerator for 30 minutes.

Divide mixture into 3 equal parts. Shape each part into a ball and roll in peanuts.

Wrap cheese balls individually in wax paper and chill in the refrigerator overnight, until firm.

Yield: 3 cheese balls

GRANOLA GOODNESS MIX

★★★★★★★★★★★★★★★★★★★★★★★★★★

2/3 cup creamy peanut butter
2/3 cup honey
1/2 teaspoon ground cinnamon
1 teaspoon vanilla
4 cups granola
1 cup raisins
1/4 cup chopped dates
1/4 cup chopped figs
1 cup peanuts

Preheat oven to 300°F.

Combine peanut butter, honey, and cinnamon in a saucepan and heat until mixture is smooth and creamy. Remove from heat and stir in vanilla and granola.

Spoon mixture into a greased 9 × 13-inch pan. Bake for 35 to 40 minutes, stirring occasionally.

Turn oven off. Mix in raisins, dates, figs, and peanuts. Let stand in unlit oven for about 1½ hours, stirring occasionally, until dry.

Store in a covered container.

Yield: Approximately 8 cups of mix

ORANGE CARROT TOAST SPREAD

★★★★★★★★★★★★★★★★★★★★★★★★★

1/2 cup creamy peanut butter
1/4 cup orange juice
1/4 teaspoon grated orange peel
2 tablespoons honey
1/4 cup raisins
1/4 cup shredded carrots

Mix together thoroughly peanut butter, orange juice, orange peel, honey, raisins, and carrots.

Yield: Approximately 1 cup spread

The four top selling brands of peanut butter in the United States and their respective shares of the total national market are as follows:

Skippy—40%
Jif—17%
Peter Pan—7%
Superman—7%

PB & FRUIT-FLAVORED POPCORN BALLS

★★★★★★★★★★★★★★★★★★★★★★★★★★★

1 cup peanut butter
3/4 cup light corn syrup
3 ounces fruit-flavored gelatin
3/4 cup granulated sugar
12 cups popped popcorn

Combine peanut butter, corn syrup, gelatin, and sugar in a saucepan and cook over low heat, stirring constantly, until mixture is melted.

Spoon over popcorn, stirring to coat completely. Let cool for 5 minutes.

Using very slightly oiled hands, shape popcorn into 1½-inch balls.

Yield: Approximately 4 dozen balls

Thirty thousand peanut butter sandwiches can be made from the peanuts grown on just one acre of land.

PB FLAPJACKS

★★★★★★★★★★★★★★★★★★★★★★★★★★★

2 cups all-purpose flour
2 teaspoons baking powder
2 tablespoons granulated sugar
1/4 teaspoon salt
2 eggs
4 tablespoons peanut butter
2 tablespoons melted butter or margarine
1 1/2 cups milk
PB Syrup (recipe follows)

Mix together flour, baking powder, sugar, and salt. Mix in eggs, peanut butter, and butter. Stir in milk.

Spoon onto a lightly greased griddle about 1/4 cup of batter for each flapjack. Cook to a golden brown, turning only once.

Top with hot syrup.

PB SYRUP

½ cup creamy peanut butter
½ cup softened butter or margarine
½ cup dark corn syrup

Combine peanut butter and butter in a saucepan and cook over low heat, stirring constantly. Gradually mix in corn syrup, blending well.

FRUIT DIP

★★★★★★★★★★★★★★★★★★★★★★★★★★

12 ounces tofu
1/2 cup creamy peanut butter
2 bananas
1 tablespoon honey
1 teaspoon lemon juice
3/4 cup strawberry yogurt
1/4 teaspoon grated orange peel

Place tofu, peanut butter, bananas, honey, lemon juice, yogurt, and orange peel into a blender and blend until dip is thoroughly mixed and smooth.

Yield: Approximately 3 cups of dip

During World War II, the Anheuser-Busch company, best known today for its Budweiser and Michelob beers, patented and produced a yeast peanut butter that was high in Vitamin D. It was one of many innovative food products developed by the company to help the war effort.

CEREAL SNACK MIX

★★★★★★★★★★★★★★★★★★★★★★★★★

2 tablespoons butter or margarine
5 tablespoons creamy peanut butter
2 cups bite-size wheat cereal
2 cups bite-size rice cereal
¹/₄ cup peanuts

Preheat oven to 375° F.

Melt butter in a large saucepan over low heat. Stir in peanut butter, mixing thoroughly. Add cereals and peanuts and stir to coat completely.

Remove from heat and spread mix on an ungreased cookie sheet. Bake for 8 to 10 minutes, until golden brown.

Drain on paper towels and let cool.

Yield: Approximately 4 cups of mix

LARRY: How can we tell if an elephant has been in our house?

HONEY: It's easy. Just look for his footprints in the jar of peanut butter.

INDEX

★★★★★★★★★★★★★★★★★★★★★★★★★★★

130